One Simp

By Paula Ginsburg

Think globally, act locally!

Illustrations by Julie Freeman
& Anka Trubnikov

To my parents, Mary and Larry Ginsburg, who
instilled in me a deep love and appreciation for
Nature and all of her gifts.

Illustrations by Julie Freeman and Anka Trubnikov
Editing and production coordination by Gideon Kramer
ISBN-10: 1461134781
ISBN-13: 978-1461134787

About the Project Behind
One Simple Thing

One Simple Thing is based on a project of the same name which began in 1990 out of Paula Ginsburg's determination to bring environmental awareness and activism to her students. For years she searched for a project that would be simple, fun, and readily visible in San Francisco neighborhoods. To her great delight, this local effort has evolved into a colorful, homegrown poster campaign involving thousands of students and hundreds of cafés in San Francisco and beyond.

While the subject of *One Simple Thing* is napkins, conserving napkins is just a symbol for something far more significant: the need to take heart and action in all of our daily habits. Making big changes can be difficult and seem overwhelming. The key is to value the *little* things we all can do each day. With more than 300 million people in this country alone, just imagine what could be accomplished if each of us focused on just one simple thing?

To learn more about the **One Simple Thing Project**, please visit Paula's blog at:

http://powerofonesimplething.blogspot.com

or e-mail her at **paula.onesimplething@gmail.com**

 **Paula Ginsburg** is a lifelong public school teacher and environmental advocate. Since 1974, she has devoted her teaching career to inspiring her students to appreciate and protect our natural world.

Paula currently resides in San Francisco's vibrant Mission District, where she can often be found in local cafés dreaming up new and innovative ways to expand the message of *One Simple Thing*.

I'm Sammy the Seagull
And this is my home.
It's called San Francisco,
and here is my poem.

It's about a few kids
who decided to do
just one simple thing
from a new point of view.

See if you can find
me in each illustration
in this book.

They learned in their school
that our planet's in trouble.
We have to take action
and start on the double.

What could they do
as a simple reminder
to help people care to
treat Earth so much kinder?

They went to the park
for a picnic and fun.
There was trash everywhere.
What could be done?

Wrappers and napkins
get tossed on the ground,
and people don't see
that their trash blows around.

It ends up in parks,
on streets and in dumps.
Just thinking about it
can give me goosebumps!

And not only that . . .
it gets even worse.
Wasting energy making this stuff
is a curse.

We've got to take action,
we've got to use less
or our beautiful city
will be a big mess.

In cafés and restaurants
where pastries are bought,
we waste lots of napkins
not giving a thought.

Dispensers are placed
on a counter or table,
and customers grab them
because they are able.

The kids watched this and wondered
and wondered how come
people took many napkins,
when they needed just one.

So they sat in their classroom
and thought of a way
to reduce what each person
discards every day.

They created some posters
and put them in places
so people might pause
before wiping their faces.

Each poster is placed
where customers read:
"Take only the napkins
that you really need."

The owners of cafés
were glad for the signs,
which make people think
upon reading their lines.

The posters are tiny
but their message implies
a lot more than only
what first meets the eyes.

The project has grown
to a symbol that stands
for *all* habits and actions
that lie in *our* hands.

Our campaign is simple,
but the lesson is great,
take care of our planet,
there's no time to wait.

Look at this city
that sits on the bay.
It's lovely and lively—
just see how we play!

Let's not take it for granted
and make no mistake,
we have to think more
about choices we make.

If you find your head spinning
with problems you see,
slow down, think it over,
the answer may be
to choose just *one* problem
and focus a bit,
seek out a buddy,
then get right to it.

Remember the changes
your actions will bring,
and remember the power
of ONE SIMPLE THING.